The Scrawny Sonnets

and Other Narratives

❧ *The Scrawny Sonnets*

Poems by Robert Bagg

and Other Narratives ⟨⟩

University of Illinois Press   *Urbana Chicago London*

Some of these poems have been published
in the following magazines:

*The Atlantic Monthly, The Massachusetts Review, Poetry,
The Hollins Critic, Quabbin, Jeopardy, Open Places,
The Far Point, Conflux, Consumption, The Mill Mountain
Review,* and *The Penny Paper.*

"Aphrodite" is reprinted from Euripides' *Hippolytos,*
translated by Robert Bagg, illustrated by Leonard Baskin,
printed at The Gehenna Press, Northampton, Mass., 1969.

"Aphrodite" is from *Hippolytos* of Euripides, translated by
Robert Bagg. © 1973 by Robert Bagg. Reprinted by
permission of Oxford University Press, Inc.

"The Living Sweetness" was first published in *Poetry
Amherst,* Amherst College Press, Amherst, Mass., 1972.

"Epidauros" was first published in *Poetry.*

for James Scully

Contents

Je demande la vie éternelle

Complacent waters kept pulling my blankets out to sea
That first morning in Paradise   and my hand worked
In my eye hollow   knuckling out
The last of the world's grit
Touching the mystery of Picasso's ladies   lopsided eyes
Around the corner from themselves   above me   a showerbath
Collapsed strange water through the walls
A laundress on a motorbike
Arrived next door at the *Villa d'aujourd'hui*
We rest on the trembling bones of the house
A great brass knocker strikes oak   below me
The blonde child Sandra   holding the long linen of her
Dress aloft in her fist
Bangs the Gorgon until her mother opens
Je demande la vie éternelle   she says
And enters then her mother's arms
And then drives off in their Dauphine
I slept   long hollow booms
Turned my benighted soul to a gentle cathedral   black
Women lit candles   softness of shoes   but the knocking could not
Be shrugged off   doors opened to Sandra   veiled   golden
I took my time walking the aisle under the blazing nave
And I asked her   *What are you doing here   my child?*
Je demande la vie éternelle   mon Père   Why
Was my hand warming hers?   Who dares give
Her shining days this passing glance
I thought   but I went through the motions
As she knelt   and the water
Danced on her hair   in a circling deluge
Whirling forth from the lawn sprinkler

I

In the seven colors of the world
As she tumbled with her Alsatian under the crowning mist
And I was steady now   woken
Watching her trying to hold her face still
For his tongue   till her mother let
That rainbow fall   spinning the faucet
Off   for the guests are coming with canapés
And sparkling wine   her damp sneakers
Scrape off   her hair revives in a towel
From the leafy chaos of the trellis   she picks grapes
With a courtesan's tenderness   on the white tablecloth
An admiral in his eightieth year   is painting Sandra
In pink champagne   she won't hold still for him
The first strokes of her hair are drying too swiftly
The admiral sets his brush down on the stone wall
Sandra is drawn off into the murmuring undertow
Her eyelids weathering a compliment
Her champagne foaming like the sea herself
Sandra shines as far from the old man now as the joys of heaven.

The Defense of the West

I am writing over my own shoulder
Suicide notes for several old friends —
Mimicking their longhand, getting the idioms right,
Doing it all on the gray of a magic slate
In whose sheen one man's script steps lightly South
Into the Nubian Desert, there to blacken of thirst.
I spare him that, tearing the cellophane free.
Whisk it dissolves, whispered scars left on the slate.

Close to the truth of a death wish
My hand turns cruel and frightened. Still,
I cannot touch their troubles except in the voice
We all save for the end. The voice I hear
Is someone least expected — he seemed sanity,
Civility and genius — their very self.
So hugely does he embrace us
He dwarfs his own words.

Dear Robert,

I suffer, suspecting how little distress
My death will cause in us all.
All my windows are shut. I need new air.
I taught you Greek, I tuned your ears,
I gave you shot after shot at the light of Southern France
And the Roman Campagna. I waited for you to grow up,
Burning to turn into you, to get inside for one second,
So we would both be moved
By the same things. You shrug and blink,
Grown deaf, as though your ears clogged at great height.
My thousand voices and the earth with many ears
Drift apart. I find myself saying to Russia almost personally:

You must believe I will kill you
Before our friendship can ever
Get off the ground, this friendship
Miraculously built from shared
Conviction of murderous intent.

My mind is the hair of Damocles
Aching to snap.

When I dwell on that explosion
In John Kennedy's head —
The mind can make no sense of such a thought.

The pressure to lend my despair
And your power to kill
To quicken the national reflex sends tremors
Shivering through those whom the surf raises, then
Surrounds with foam, those with blown minds,
Those adrenalin addicts who drive their obsessions

Like cars at the limits of adhesion,
Those getting dressed half-awake
Sensing the dawn's earliest nuclear insinuation;
It takes it out of me, so much fatigue
Like a slowly dissolving marriage
Dissolves me from the murder I must
And no longer wish to promise . . .

I stopped him at this point, letting his
Unspoken words drop
Down the bottomless well of my ear.
They tumble in soundless nothing —

My stylus strikes through his message.
When I put his words
Behind bars, the bars pulse and vibrate.

It is time to strip the cellophane free,
Which crinkles like skin coming off,
His words losing themselves in sudden transparency
A glossy and vacant moment
Through which the unscathed world comes calmly back
Demanding to be seen.

Sappho

Although I didn't say so then,
I want quite honestly to die.
She's gone, and there were a lot
Of tears when she said, *Can you*
Still feel how we touched each other,
Sappho — I hate leaving you.
Don't you see (I said) listen,
Why not leave radiant
As if you remembered the
Honey of it? Why make me tell you
Things you can't have forgotten?
How lazy and sensual we were,
Busy with headbands of violets
Roses crocuses — all you bunched
In rings and piled over me,
Silly necklaces full of silky
Petals, slippery damp on my
Soft neck. And your palms, wet with
Rare royal myrrh shampoo, would
Massage and rinse out my lovely hair . . .

(after Lobel-Page 94)

Zibbie

Summer slammed behind us. Mossy carpets
In the moviehouse soothed my bare soles. Her arms
Where sun had soaked deep   savored the oncoming glow
I sit peeling toe-callus, excruciating, in quick tugs.
Her lips spread soft and wincing
For an ice-cold tuft of fountain water.
On waterskis skimming the lobby mirrors
Our time-killing eyes collided with each other's bodies.
She sucked her lazy belly in
Where my unease bruised
Then arched up on her toes,   to dive recklessly.
Under my own feet that supple springboard
Held a resilient wallop. I glided off.
She coming next hit the jarred board badly,
Chin jammed when the locked knees can't give in.

Out burst children from the movie's side
Burbling around and through us;
When the tide turned undertow pulled us to our seats
From whose velour we watched until celluloid
Gathered its people into tight circles and its tail slapped
Free of a huge oblong of great white light.
Then off the Whip to the House of Thrills where snakes of air
Fought her skirts with a flurry of punches.
When I tugged she was a sea-anchor in the swift night.
Bulbous Dionysian mirrors pulled me like taffy, in two,
Zibbie burst into tears.
                              As always, apart
I shivered in her gentle hysterical grip.
Fresh walls of sinuous glass

Bloomed her slight breasts out of hand, she wrenched
Loose from a fifty months' pregnancy to let her real
Troubles fill her like popcorn which we watched
Explode into fluff from a hard kernel.

If we sat too long in one spot
Black breakers retrieving their white souls
Crept up to us.
                    Huger and number
Than ever in my life walking out
My feet soar heavily off the bottom, whose

Swirling spirits massage my ankles.
Out bumps a chunk of air from my trunks,
Queering my belly on its upward glide. Zibbie
Wades toward me and the salt sea running in
Leaves her stinging
Rocking a maimed murmur *Oh it hurts me*.
I went under for long as my lungs held out;
Surfaced, my stuffed ears warble with her screamlets,
Little mammals sprinting crazy on the swell
Where my head floats. I whack my temple and a little warm
Water trickles my cheek, that my ears may open now
On the inhuman quiet of the Jersey shore.

John Moore's Muse

Bitch-mistress of the blank mind and the migraine,
Of shoulders paralyzed from psyche
Down to fingerquick — you wind your holy promise
Of human light in sinewed strangleholds

Where inkling ambushes idea and truth
Is a gordian quart of black ink.   Set free
And give way to your servant, John Moore,
Who won't, like Alexander, murder

Our monstrous knot, but would justly conquer you.
In fine strands from his deep well let him unwind
What binds him to you, as once you heard him,
With a curse, speak Sophocles' quietness;

Now let him hold in his own hands
Priam's hands, just as these held
Achilles' man-killing hands,
That John's hand may move as his mind moves.

The Eighteenth Book

— for Martin Kligerman (1936-70)

Marty's life. It was touched by the *Iliad*
On a stony hillside pasture
In Tyringham, Massachusetts in June '57.
A week before graduation
We picnic after rehearsing *Nausicaa.*
Green Maiden is with us (her name in the play)
She will drive south to Fire Island
In twenty minutes; a car is stashed for her
In a Safeway parking lot.
We admire the momentum building in her life.
"Green Maiden" says Marty, so reckless
We cringe for him
"May I rest my head in your lap?"
She's silent   then seems to answer
Chillingly more than he asked
Just this once she says and his head
Goes down to her lap
A brief glorious while

Just that once   his buried wrath
Demanded of her who knew   how much life
How much life   the gods
Would let him have

Playing the Wheel in Juan

We are leaving the Casino at Juan-les-Pins
   The roulette marbles still tumbling over numbers
    About to lodge in somebody else's stomach.

By a hotel full of the Rolling Stones
   Arrogantly parked is a black Maserati,
    The mild velleity of its transparent fastback

Frosted smooth by the August dawn.
   There a suave finger — speaking, I supposed,
    For the whole woman — had written,

"Dear Luc, I waited for you here since three hours.
   Your anger not incurable anger?
    Biot 479 310"

My fingers are spinning the dial
   Around like the wheel of fortunate numbers
    Ticking into a perfect parlay

Just as she answers — Daisy! with a voice
   Full of money which I spend in the dream
    Je suis Luc   J'arrive J'arrive

The Scrawny Sonnets

Staying

In town a week   knowing dimly you are here
I find your rooms   you're gone   but our old friend
In jeweled gloom stands lost on your stoop
We are bees hovering cheeseclothed honey
You've drawn him to the brink of female love
And strand him there   *I can't give him balls*
Evasive when I finally find you home
If he makes it with me then we're both cool.

Last time we knew you   you were faery child
Bony vehement mocker of passion
Now your scrawny queenly self   doubles our
Bewilderment   we love sometimes the girl
Sometimes the boy in you   *I'm glad you're staying*
You say   who's loved in you not your affair.

Damp Cashmere

Out of damp sneakers and stiff rainy hair,
Blue jeans and brown cashmere, I revive you:
In those days *très très sage,* sniffing the unfair
Intoxications your dank self would brew,
Scrawny prophet of the girl you grew into.
All your wiry might resists that brash whore —
So much so I brace me for *her,* not you,
Prickly, elusive, tremblesome and pure.

Tonight I hold that mildewed negative,
Taken of you naked, sucking some pears.
You gave it away, safe in your black hue.
That oath I swore never to develop you
I break now, steeping you in the small hours,
Playful darkness gone and swelling up alive.

Quiet

Your liner leaves this afternoon for France.
I arrive at eight sharp. Though we're not Friends
We'll go to Quaker Meeting just this once.
Too Late you yell to your sister, who sends
Me somewhere else. The loud shower on your back
Pounds you with warmth, you rub it in. I'm in shock
But go anyway to the Quaker's quiet
And sit through it, wondering why it is so sweet.

Cold years after France I drop you at a friend's.
My car quits. No answer when I walk back
Looking for a phone. A shower ceases and sends
Warmth which, found, is a cool spring. You don't shock
But say over and over as your quiet
Dries into skin and words: *Why is it so sweet?*

Divine Wind

She's at the wheel, and she resists each tree,
Telephone pole, oncoming car; knuckles grim
Against her Divine Wind, her burning kamikaze.
Trees howl at her to crash and sleep with them.

She says: "I love trees, but they are all killers.
It is marvelous to go very fast."
So we graze that mobilized army of hers.
"There's kamikaze in you too" — she gives me a blast

Of her eyes — "You'd smash your life at me. You're doom
Loving, I'm swift and glorious disaster —
Right now you're in flames and there's no flying home.
I'm your new life." As proof, she wrenches her car
At limbs who would maul my skull. We're skidding
Through a Rest Stop. As we kiss: "I wasn't kidding."

Black Coffee

A knock tensed us. Our room is under siege.
Please don't breathe. Lacking a wall to climb
On my shoulders she froze her strangled rage —
Her unsuppressible sigh laid bare the room.
ALL RIGHT FOR YOU. He camped outside her door.
Pluck of his fingers and excluded lips
Coolly *tutoying* her on his guitar
Struck her into scrunched, humiliated shapes,

Then tossed a last strum to the Cambridge air.
A car door clunks shut, billows of white exhaust.
That voice left her hair drenched, her skin phosphor.
She showers suddenly and gets bleakly dressed,
Brewing relentless mugs of black coffee
Whose sternness stares from us until five-thirty.

Getting Killed

"He eased into my coffeesulk at Bicks
As though I were a weird piranha river —
Not a true suicide, more as a lover
Courts brutal fingernails to give him kicks.
Scenes from your sex life ripped him to the bone.
Each strange lay sends waves of grinning torpor
Swirling out his stirring fingers. Pouring sugar
He drowns his coffee in one crumbling dune."

"Once he smashed in my door. I opened his tight
Clenched face, but wouldn't screw. He left less hope-
Less, but then climbed my roof, pried the skylight
Over my tub (me in it, slimed with soap)
Dangling, then letting drop, so the bath sprawled.
I loved him. It was just like getting killed."

Let It Ring

On fifty feet of tense extension cord
You and a phone vanish behind a stair
As under a shower.   His roaring fondness poured
Liquids I couldn't hear. Talced, fresh and fair

You reappear — the drained receiver lolls
On its curved spine,   his once extinguished moan
Thrashes to life under your tongue,   then fails
And is obliterated by the dial tone.

"I'm going, he's in one of his suicidals."
I slam my way across to your bookshelf.
You say firmly from your caressing towels,
"Nobody loves anybody ever,   enough."
Crane Brinton's *History of Western Morals*
Begs like a phone book to be torn in half.

Too Much

"The people I live with down here divorce
Sue each other   take knives to their kids
Pound doors   pass out   vomit   stab their veins   when things
Deteriorate. My quiet is from coming — though
No quiet is ever enough. I am too much
For just sex. You're safe, at least to yourself.
What happens when you take me? you calmly
Embalm me — my body is malleable
To you — I turn into wife, or something
Bourgeoise, like poems, or pain you can handle.
I hadn't seen John for a month, or made love
To a soul — my face was all oily, dammed up.
John lit with pleasure, and said, 'Poor girl, poor cunt,
You've fallen behind. You'll never catch up.' "

Plenty

"The cool ones pile sandals and vine leaves and lots
Of words outside my door. One stuffs my ice-box
With citrus — dollars drift into my life,
I'm cold fall rain stripping their brilliant trees.

When he left me, one boy gave me a list —
Twelve Harvard Professors, each one willing
To keep a girl. I have holes in my life.
My friends fill them and then I empty again."

Words please themselves when they're involved with her.
Yes fills with self-love. *Body* grows fur.
I open *whore* and oranges fall on me.
Plenty makes me ache softly in the balls.
Her hand's on them and on my mouth. She senses
I am about to say *cat* and then *wife*.

Cat

Sleep lifts, a shopping bag crinkles and bulges;
Mewing, she muscles her white fur in; contained;
Loving it. When I launch out of bed she's there,
Cat in an arch of pleasure, grazing my shin.
My hand pummels and reverses her grain
Until fur reeks of you though you still sleep.
The cat's out of the bag and the sky's torn —
Two feet of snow have fallen overnight,

Its fresh white depth rubs against our warmth,
So vast a trophy fur we wonder who
Subdued it to this sullen animal
Who resists and pleasures our moving through it,
Who shuts the city down,   whose seventh life
Is icy treachery as I drive its roads.

Wife

She drops a lobster into the misty pot;
Black eyes go under and slender hawsers
Feeling death. Filling jars from the kettle
The rising note tells her exactly when

To stop. She wakes to something gently scraping,
Spasski's paw in the gerbil cage she says
And rises. When she comes back she smells my hair
And sweater, turns on light and reads mysteries.

When I wake the lamp is still on. She's gone.
Out by the fir trees and the rose garden
She sits naked and haunted in the grass,
Her book open, wind and moon churning its pages.
Her knees point North. Her vertebrae are wet.
She says with white breath   *How does it come out?*

Trompe l'âme

The Children of Leda

'My father coughs behind me in the house.
The children tremble against the sea.
The entire world is real.'

The thought is a dove launched from an ark.

Real, like a willing labyrinth, whose kiss
Blocks the way to her love
But the kiss rolls away
As your mind recedes into its powers
And the dove finds the world
The loved person   terra cognita   still wet
And shining from our own recent thought.

Real, but uninhabitable
For who lives there
Who even comes close
Only those restrained men
Who keep their distance   grown strong
In their folly   taking in the world
Until its joy undoes them.

When father coughs
The children tremble
They can stand it   this dissolving
Promise of the precarious   but if *you*

Edge into the heart of that scene
You're a shivering child   wave upon wave
Suppresses your father's cough
The sea mouths your cold feet

You hold nothing back   ruthlessly
Blindfolded by confusion and tears.
A reassuring hand will then touch off
Your lemmings   your blind loves
Possessed by dispossession
Your eyes leave home

When they reach Europe
The feast of art surrounds them like a room.

Something sensational happens in the walls

A woman wakes from someone else's sleep   legs redden
Plunging an intestinal mountain of grapes
A man's vile life bursts into flame inside him.
Though you are wholly inside the room
Its walls suck the life out of you   you see it set
Fresh in the ever-healing fresco

Her hands barely touching the swan's surging neck
Leonardo's Leda strokes into the mind of Zeus
Unquenchable adoration   we feel Zeus
Conceiving us   we're Leda's children
A shell forms around us we can't crack
We are unborn   we're up against
The honesty of frescoes   their solid wall
Their unacceptable invitation
To Paradise
To the Triumph of Bakkhos
To the Last Judgment

Enormous invisible pressure holds us
Still and poised   *Trompe l'oeil*
The eye is stunned
The world's composed.

But the day comes
When the deceit of beckoning facades
Touches us farther in than composure reaches
And perspective no longer
Puts us in our
Place.

Rembrandt's Dust

Therefore it happened while living at the Villa
La Gardiole on the Cap d'Antibes
I wished to be free of the Muse
To elude her tactile deceptions
And her laws of perspective   the ones
Even Picasso
Kept by mocking.

I wanted to be free of those rhythms
Commandeering small talk with grand finesse
So words could vanish as I spoke them
At their own speed
Like other living things.

Mme Cornelius became my instructress in
Passionate defection — ex of the Ziegfield Follies
Living divorced in the palace of a scandinavian king
Cooking pasta in gold lamé pajamas.
When we were silenced
By her huge Gobelins of the Annunciation
She opened portfolios of her master drawings.
One a Rembrandt:
Sketches of a scorched face
Over a classical nude in the lower corner;
Various severed and violent limbs.
Did we doubt it? She stunned us: *Of course
It's real. Look.* She erased at the man's chin —
His stubble, his character
Crumbled into black rubber
Which she blew away.

That was her answer. Breathe art
When it becomes your pride
With your own breath into oblivion.

Her breath is almost imperceptible, like
The vodka and *amour propre* it sustains;
But she has the authority,
Dispersing Rembrandt's dust through her salon,
Of the goddess herself,
The Muse gone quietly promiscuous, never again
To deliver her grace to a poet.
She gives herself away — out of sight, beyond words.
She makes herself abundant, overruns cities,
Three billion people cannot exhaust her —
And she will never in this life gather
Powerfully into a poem.

After she blows through us all

What is the *Iliad* but a cloud of atomic particles
Fallen on a Thracian encampment
Whose fighters are possessed — they love death, they are
Terrifying to themselves and their enemies,
Herons
Riding enormous thermals of murder.

Milton, when Blake shakes him awake,
Looks through humanity for his lost wives,
His lost poems, and comes to them
Sighing — they are profoundly loved
By angels with phalluses sensitive as wings,
Their minds sweet as the wind from Oololon.

Picasso Music

Calm beams from the Antibes lighthouse
Strike water brighter than our skins.
Ankles collect in a swell, then one
Apollonian breast made of black water
Finishes pale and crestfallen
Darkness spirits away
Salt-crusted earthly hair, mist
From dissonant waves falls upon us,
A hissing Picasso music. Quietly
Coming ashore,   no glow aboard us.
Picasso had broken our bones.
They never mend.

We try to re-enter our shivering lives.
Everyone lending a hand, we slide towels
Around limbs and through buttocks
Rub each other's hair into a slight dampness.

Soft Names

Swimming is within   the darkness out there
A party in Cannes five hours off
We immerse numb under enormous towels
Whoever tries to make sense   fatigue will set
His each phrase free
From its drowsy neighbor
Person from person dissolves
We are primates no more
Our reverie is water gazelles
Rubbing haunches with grazing Ferraris
Grazing the *moyenne corniche*

Whose headlights pick up
Our decelerating walls

Someone unseen   perhaps Claudine
Is rolling her bikini up
Into one ball   we hear rough strife
Her sweetness crushed
A sodden globe of maltreated seawater
Quieting to a few drops   which drip
As she walks anywhere   like a wish   touching
Us who breathe unaware towards sleep
Her fingers questioning our nape hair
Breath setting off gentle spinal explosions
Her footsoles   sex   inner forearms
Crossing our own   we cannot tell her
Whom the mountains skied into hardness
The summer into seamusk
From the eventful darkness

A hand awaits her nearing face
Both lost   bats in a black mind
Who never touch   life's pulse
Beats alone in its own wrist
Informing itself   like Keats
Easeful darkness is what we love
Soft names calling for her   *White Negress*
Bête Noire   Seamouth   touch us with this
Kiss from nowhere
Which the insane return

By morning her body has turned white
She is the last to wake
Her sleeping sex is darkness visible
She lifts coffee   everything
Black
Disappears within her lips
Where she is   who she has loved
Just dawning
On her dun skin.

The Living Sweetness

A girl dissolved in the night or in surf
Will glow in the spiritual dark
Encourage our lives to dissolve into poems
Secure and insolent there as drowned sailors
Revived desolate among sirens.

More often though we're on the way out
With Scott Fitzgerald
Immersed in the streetlights between neighboring harbors
His power distilling the living sweetness
Into little lines in books
But wanting like a saint the miracles he felt
To transform him instead.

World would not do this.
He'd seen Verdun   where empires lunged like lovers
And turned one another
Into a million bloody rugs.

At the Hotel Residence du Cap
He came in from the gin-battered patio
As if he had seen the lion of passion block the mountain
He was ready to climb
Certain the stars were moved by love
Wondering
When lion and stars would seize his life.
Nicole he cured; Zelda died in flames.

Trompe l'âme

She is what happens to us.
She gives pain and sweetness
Almost beyond our power to feel.

And when it's over
We live through her breathing
As though she were the south coast of France.

Out open windows of my groundfloor study
I see her coming. Her dachshunds wallow
Over my sill, curt
On a chariot leash.
Nora in jodhpurs holds them
Skating on red tile.
"You don't need to make smalltalk with me."

"Don't you think," she says anyway,
"*The Sun Also Rises* a dumb book?"
She'd known a chap who had his
Blown off in the war, like Jake,
But hired a surgeon to model him
Five platinum new ones — she'd seen
The rack in his bedroom.

He sinks in —
This man becoming his own thought
We feel all metaphor suddenly harden
We're high on the lighthouse
Moonfloor stomping and dancing
Back to ripe slime the grapes we've drunk

Later a rill out of the Admiral's wrist
Bumps into tumblers and makes port, where ride
His battlecruiser running south
From Jutland and his lost schooner
Running wine to the Cyclades.
Both gone when the wine drains.
A tower of twelve blue Gauloises packs, piled askew,
Stands near his daughter Claudine's
Color photo on the mantle;
Naked breasts and belly, polynesian brown.
Her hands reach to part
Palmfuls of yellow hair.

"There are two men I shall seek out in Hell"
The Admiral tells me, "Byron and Caligula.
Incestuous bastards."
I am fascinated by her hair.

Claudine comes home from Whiskey à Go-Go,
Her bar stool there a roulette
Grazing the eyes at cocktail hour,
The winner's balls waiting for her
To slow down   but combo numbers throb out the night
In an infinite series — no winner.

Garçons on motorbikes skid sideways outside us,
Rev insanely, demanding in the moonlight.
She won't elope.
The Admiral lunges in the slow motion of age
Brandishing ski poles   jamming spokes.
The pack is driven from *l'allumeuse Anglaise*
In a tantrum of gear changes
Down the coast road.

"The child has bums like ripe honeydew melon."
"Like ripe me," in her noon martini. We sense
Honeydew sliding into satin-soft
Pages of *Holiday*, as she dives
Ever lower under the limbo bar,
Pelvis all tension   breasts smoothed like sand dunes.

Nine hundred K's to the north
The index finger of Courrèges
Traces a curve under her navel, there
Her trousers ride, holding her
As someone alive in a hammock.
A massive sulk in Brigitte Bardot's life
Takes Claudine's hair by surprise
Matting its turbulence to cowed straw;
I drive her to Nice
Where she weighs in for stewardess
On the scales of Pan Am.
The needle leaps,
Praising her true worth to the skies,
Then wilts — she's
Overshot by a whole kilo.

Following
That morning down a dis-
Appearing path
Into a *trompe l'âme*
Was like walking through a wall
Into the next room.
She's there.
Deep in the house the Aga Khan
Departs like youth itself. The Admiral
Counterattacks
From his study:
Has that Nigger left yet?

I can tell how excited you are.
I'll feel your pulse.
Not the one trapped in your wrist.
That one I count with my fingers.
First her mouth held the pulse
Then taking it into her body
Her body counted   then lost count
It's an infinite pulse   she was saying
Long after the pulse stopped
Turning me into her.

Tu penses

I thought I was as close to the pulse of life
As I would ever go.
I was wrong.

"Tomorrow we shall cross a huge water."
"*Tu penses.*"

Claudine stands in skis on the beach
Braced for the skidding ride —
A boy falls from the stern
As the speedboat accelerates,
Its prop crushes his leg at the knee.
She pulls him to the surface
Then on to the deck
Making a tourniquet of her suit,
Stiffening blood in us all.
The owner gave her his boat.

In the days following
When my eyes touched her breasts,
My blood lunging safe,
I persuaded the body for a few strange weeks
— Itself a phallus thriving on pleasure —
Into companies of the rich,
Into lucid perishable friendships
Enormous with confidence
Keen in clothes, asleep in the sun.

A mild *tu penses* blown from the sidelong Café
Delivers a delight
It takes the whole fucking body
A lifetime to exhaust.

Aphrodite

The power I possess is sex, passion, love,
Which you mortals, in honoring me,
Celebrate in your diverse ways.
I'm no less the darling of heaven.
I am the goddess Aphrodite.
My subjects live in the Mediterranean sunlight
From the Black Sea to the Atlantic beaches
And those responsive to my sacred privileges,
My whims, my implacable caresses, I reward;
I delight them; but I stir up trouble
For any who ignore me, or belittle me,
And who do it out of stubborn pride.
Does it surprise you that gods are passionate,
That they like mortals to honor them?
If you will listen to this story
The truth of my words is quickly proven.
There lives in this province of Trozen
Hippolytos, the illegitimate child
Of Theseus and his Amazon mistress.
The old king of this province,
Pittheus the Pure, made him his protegé.
Now this young man, alone
Among his contemporaries,
Says freely I am a despicable goddess.
Marriage is anathema to him,
He goes to bed with no girl.
The goddess he adores is Artemis, a virgin,
Apollo's sister, the daughter of Zeus.
Our young friend thinks *her*
Kind of divinity the most exhilarating.

In the pale green forest they are inseparable,
They drive their killer hounds until the wildlife,
Squirrels as well as stags, is extinct.
Such a friendship between human and god
Is a remarkable event —
I would not deny him this happiness.
I have no reason to.
                              It's purely his
Offenses against me which I resent
And will punish — today.
The revenge I have planned is now ready
To emerge with no further effort from me.
These are the things already done.
Once, as he passed through Athens
On his way to see and enact
The sacred mysteries at Eleusis,
His father's wife, the matchless Phaedra,
Saw him and soon was inflamed,
In her eyes, in the soft depth of her being,
By all the insistent sexual longing
I could exert. This was my plot.
So enamoured was she,
Even before coming to Trozen,
She built a stone temple, in my honor,
Not far from the shrine of Pallas Athene.
From that slope Phaedra could look across water
To Trozen, since love was there, deep
Within that strange perspective.
Later, when Theseus fled the country,
Where he had murdered a great man's sons,
Defiling himself so badly Athens dared not
Keep him — he elected to spend
His exile-year in this country.

So it is here in Trozen that Phaedra,
Groaning dismally, her mind turbulent
Under the lash of continual lust
Fades into a wretched silence.
She has no intimate who can see or cure
What lies at the heart of this sickness.
But her love must not linger in this impasse —
Which dissolves as my plans take shape.
The real facts I will force on Theseus,
The explosion will be public.
That youth who crosses me must die.

(from Euripides' *Hippolytos*)

Dionysos

We have left Asia and forsaken
   Tmolus, our holy mountain.
      Our energy goes
To the bull god's hard sweet work,
   To his sensuous exhaustion.
      Bakkos is joy.

Anyone still on the street
   Go quietly in out of sight.
      Stay in your dark house.
         Speak nothing discordant,
Keep an immaculate silence.
   Our hymn has in it
      The living Dionysos.

That man is serene
   Who learns miracles from the god,
      Who learns *Bakkos*.
God's guidance determines his life.
He's blessed who finds Bakkos in us
   He enters our *holy body*
Purifying old lives on the mountain,
   Dancing into power
The violent mind of Bakkos.

That blessed man will touch and enact
   Cybele's secrets, the Earth Mother's
      Inviolable celebrations,
And he will travel — once ivy
   Swirls in his hair —
Slashing aloft his natural wand,
   Serving god.

Act! Bakkantes, you women
　　Who cry out for ecstasy,
Bring home the loud demon to Thebes,
　　He is the son of Zeus.
Bring him from the Phrygian mountains
　　Into the wide streets of Greece.
　　　　Restore that god to his home

Whose pregnant mother
　　Lightning stunned into labor —
　　　　Her contractions were sacred,
　　　　　　Unbearable,
Because she wished to make love
　　To pure Zeus.
　　　　She bears our god,
An unformed foetus out of her womb,
　　Then dies, loved by the lightning
　　　　With passionate savagery.

But the swift reach of Zeus
　　Assumed his son
To his secret childbearing recess,
　　Hid him there, golden pins
Closing the flesh of his thigh around him,
　　Invisible to Hera.

When the Fates had perfected
　　This bull-horned god,
　　　　Zeus bore him, then crowned him:
　　　　A supple mass of snakes
Which to this hour inspires
　　All women the god maddens
To braid into their own rich hair
　　Slithering beasts
Which their hands lift from the earth.

Put on your crown of ivy, Thebes,
  Town where Semele flowered,
Appear with green bryony's
  Delicate red berries
Blooming out of your clothes.
Your grip on branches of oak and fir
  Guides you into us:
  Our holy turmoil of Bakkos.
Loop round your brownflecked
  Fawnskinned body
A sash rippling with curls
  Of soft bright wool.

Your strong wands will vibrate with outrage —
  Use them with reverent
    Restraint.
Soon the people will dance into us,
And the man who guides our body of joy —
  That man will be the bull god
    Hounding us to Citheron —
Mountain where females sit
  Expectant and tense,
Free now of shuttles
  And their taut looms
Because Bakkos stampedes
  Their minds into madness.

  On the island of Crete's
  Holy Zeus-bearing hills
Curetes live in their cloistered ravines;
And in caves there, massive helmeted Corybantes
  First stretched
  Resilient skin
Over drums, keeping a hard dancing beat.

44

        The soft-voiced airs
        Breathed by Phrygian flutes
Climb the beat of this drum
        Given to Rhea,
        Mother of us all,
Now it's her drumbeat
        Whose pulse gives form
To the Bakkantes'
        Huge cries of joy.

Inheriting it
        From our Great Mother's care,
            Hysterical satyrs
            Found in the drum
New vigor for their festivals,
        Biennial riots
            Dionysos adores.

In the mountains Bakkos is welcome
        As he enters the Maenad —
Out of the body ravenous for joy
        She drops to the earth,
Her fawnskin sacred around her,
        She takes a goat in her hands
        Whose throat tears,
        Whose blood warms hers,
Then as the joy of her mouth
        Fills with his pulse
She is shot in terrible joy
Back to the stunning mountains
        Of Phrygia and Lydia,
And the man crying her on
        Roars into godhood
And joy bursts from her lungs.

Beneath her the meadow goes lush —
  Running with milk
  Running with wine
Running slowly with the nectar of bees.

    And the man turned god,
    Turned Bakkos himself,
  Raises aloft the fiery pine
  Whose smoke is Syrian incense.
    Running and wavering
    He bleeds behind him
    Rich red sparks and milky smoke,
  Spreading fury through frightened Maenads,
  Cutting their flesh with shrieks of sacred
    Summons,
    Ripping
  The high mountain air
  With his extravagant curls.

Now bulling through the Maenads'
    Rising joy comes the god's roar:
    "Brilliant Bakkantes! you glitter yet
  With our holy mountain's torrents of gold.
    Let Dionysos pound
    In your dancing leaps
      And your singing,
  Let him pound in the drums'
      Report.
  Pour glory upon him.
    The joy of your voices
      Inspires his large rich voice.
  Do it with Phrygian bellows
    And rallying cries."

Then the tones flowing holy
  From hollow lotusflutes
    Thunder harmonies to pace
Blithe spirits of the women seen traveling
  Far out on the mountain.
    The mountain!

Like a yearling grazing near its mother
  The Bakkant strikes her limbs
    Into brief lightning-
      Like strides.

(from Euripides' *Bakkhai*)

Epidauros

Le poète doit être capable de tout

— COCTEAU

1.   The Road

The road does not think   the road
lifts who walks it out of the valley
shares his exhaustion and blows dry his sweat
contracts his disease and sucks the poison
into the wind and olive roots
it lets him in to what it knows
it knows Epidauros and it cures
those who relinquish to its grip

as it creases the brown palm a lifeline opens
through the clenched Peloponnesus
telling Greece its own fortune
bees from their wooden hives
still sift savage pollen of Kypris
on all our flowering fields
jugular fissures between cliffs
swallow all travelers   ancient trucks
with whom I hitch rides
shudder to crests which set us free
in colder air the movie star McQueen
overtakes me   his body vibrating from
power he sits astride
                  we smoke
                        he banks
into loops of descending road
                            from deep in my head

against the bridge of my nose   Pasiphae at last
braces her feet as she swells to the boneless
murder of the bull's orgasm
its mythical rage now a soft pulse   her
hysterical delicacy lost on him

2.   The Disease of Images

There are images made of roads who meet
where legs come together at the body
these put the eyes out   they lead eyes
who love the naked mother
to the steel pins of her brooch
imagination blinds you   like your own father it's
capable of anything   stops at nothing
it sucks your life into one image   let it be
a word from Apollo
or lightning from Zeus
it wipes out
how many?   every blessed
modality of your life
and at Colonnus
the loving earth receives you
she is your mother
you hear musical wrath from your own body
filling the whole woman with child

3.   Arrival

I walk in the good hands of the road
which let me go in a meadow
the road fleetingly a river
flowing through ruins on the valley floor

I make flames for coffee
in the evening sadness of nothing coming on
it is the god of nothingness   whose blackness
annihilates its own stimulants
the patient cup still warms my hands
and rest invites my journey to flow
sweetly back through my body
does this fatigue of walking
lead somewhere images cannot find
if I follow the body
as one follows a road into the mountains?

Without warning   I become what I climb
the road and the olive tree
with the mildest encouragement from mist
collecting on my hair and eyelids
my eyes blink open as olives   black
wizen-glistening with digestive acid

4.   The Cult of Asklepios

Greeks bring their sickness
from mainland and island to these precincts
sacred to Asklepios   student of the natural body
student of herbs
Cheiron the centaur taught him to heal
those to be cured are made pure by a cold sea bath
incense fumes permeate them
they sacrifice to the god cakes gorged with honey
a rigorous fast prepares them to receive

their new selves   they dress in white
the dream-inducing color
sleep in long houses lit all night with small lamps

snakes slide through the sleepers
whispering sometimes a cure in their ears
in natural dreams the soul reveals
what will enhance the body
at dawn priests in white gowns circulate
with sacred dogs   with ointments
the uncured remain   to act in the great theater
run in games at the stadium
if sickness persists or death comes
the patient thereby declares his impiety
incurable failure of confidence
it is not permitted mortal man
to die or be born in these precincts

One paralyzed in the fingers came mocking his chances
dreamed he played dice with a god
who stomped
on guilty fingers which woke flexing

Kleo pregnant five years felt the god's hand
on the child asleep in her sleeping womb
in the morning beyond the precinct
she bore in agony a boy who washed off blood
of his own birth and walked beside his mother

5.   Sound

What in this place
precipitates wisdom from dreams
humankindness from gods and beasts?
I move in the healing valley
hearing the purity all sound
carries
the theater

immersing its tuned bowl
of stone tiers in a large bowl of hills
wherein all barking   wind modulation
the sharp spoken word   hold firm   ripen
warm mile-off animal breathing
bristles the beard from its soft sleep in my face
the khaki mound on my shoulders slides
under surveillance from the roadside
in Greek crippled by twenty centuries
what some rough shepherd is telling wells into sense
carnivorous menace running through his voice
don't sleep in this valley
wild dogs will awaken you

6.   Dogs

I shrugged him off
through sparse darkening ruins
scouting the level terrace where I would sleep
back down in that panorama of sickness and health
of blackening greens   of wounded sound growing well
salvation   say votive scratches on a wall

is an animal quietly present in dreams

I think of a hard child carried from Thebes
deranged   seething   who finds himself next morning
looking at the sick in Spartan calm
a gazelle in his arms

I am surrounded by eiderdown
cold
rain
darkness
up to my ears and eyes

Something wild
perseveres toward my smell
my knife is out
invisibly near me a sheepdog edges in
but the imagined menace
ends   he curls
into himself an inch from my scalp
limbs which monsters in halfsleep chomp away
are restored
his sleepless fur rubs me whole
his teeth   the tuneless numbness of the rain
the terrible intimacy of the valley   removed sleep
to something promised by the next world

The wind was blowing my fear
away toward the bells of sheep
hemmed in to their folds by an unseen power
then all the bells fell silent
across the floor of the Hadean valley
heaving toward me
the breath of sprinting dogs
                                    their barks
hit all around me
the sheepdog woke across my throat
for a second my face buried in fur
he crashed downhill
slowed the arriving dogs
poised their reconnaissance
returned them scrambling to lower terraces
incited again through laurel and olive
they hurl and tangle
in his arrogance

light comes and quiet comes
his jaws pulse from exertion
who is he   who gave him to me
I feel for the last waves of my disease
the dregs my cure

7.   Cure

All night whatever the valley held   washed
into my ears
                        trucks churning up
pebbles   a slow reversal of air going nowhere
the bells   the barks   singers
seeking the high notes of pleasure
responding to a radio
protective sniffs of the dog
these surfaced in my palms
which were still palms folding my gear
when I look out across it   my mind
opens into that valley   lives
beyond its own reach
welcomes all who invade it
brings all terrors near —
the god in that dog
and in those wolves
what were my sins

I leave the valley
with my eiderdown encumbered
by thirty pounds of rain
which the sun grows thirsty for

pouring lightness on my shoulders